Sweet Treats Coloring Book

by Paula Mazzoli

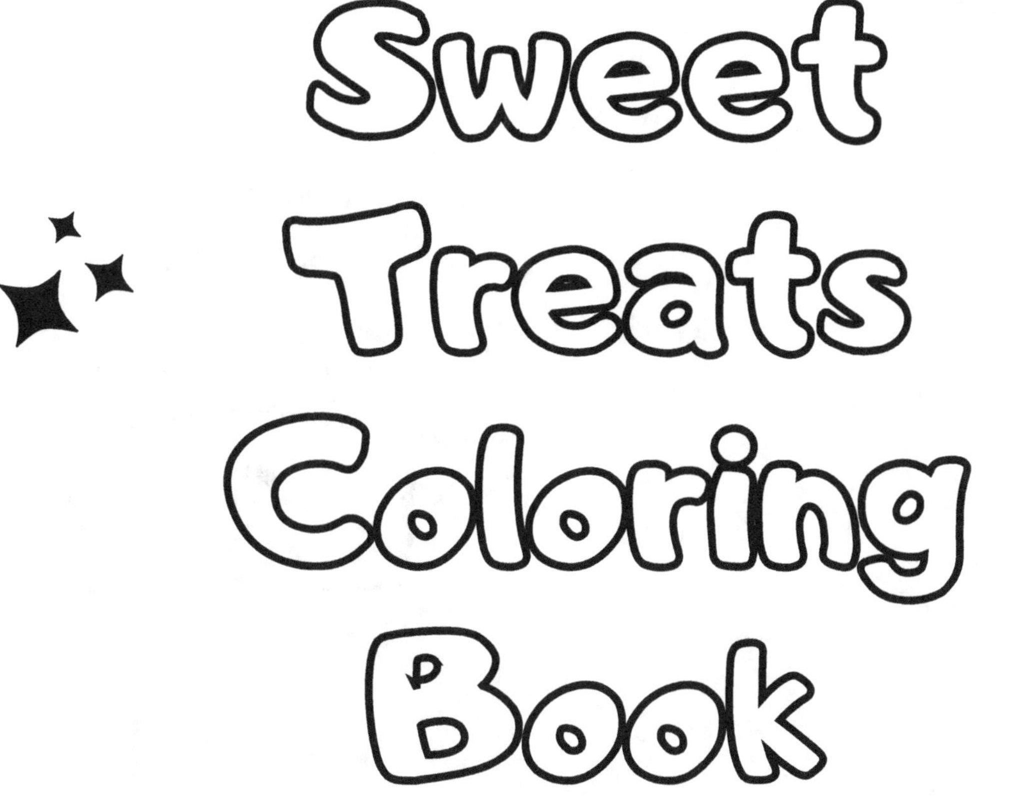

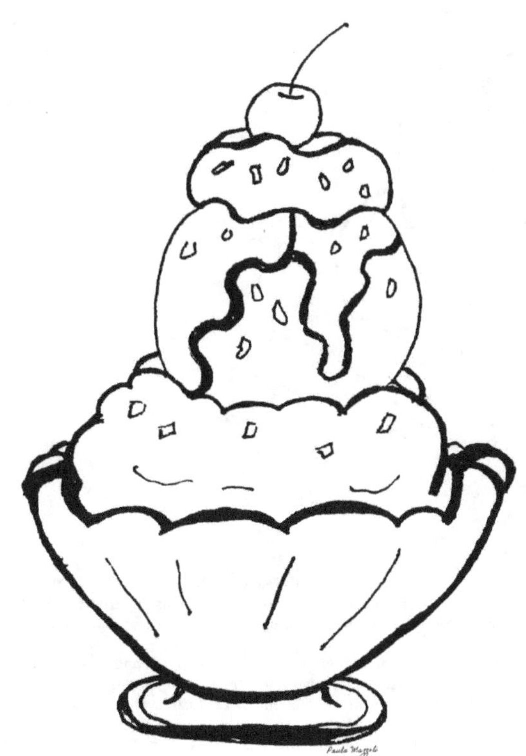

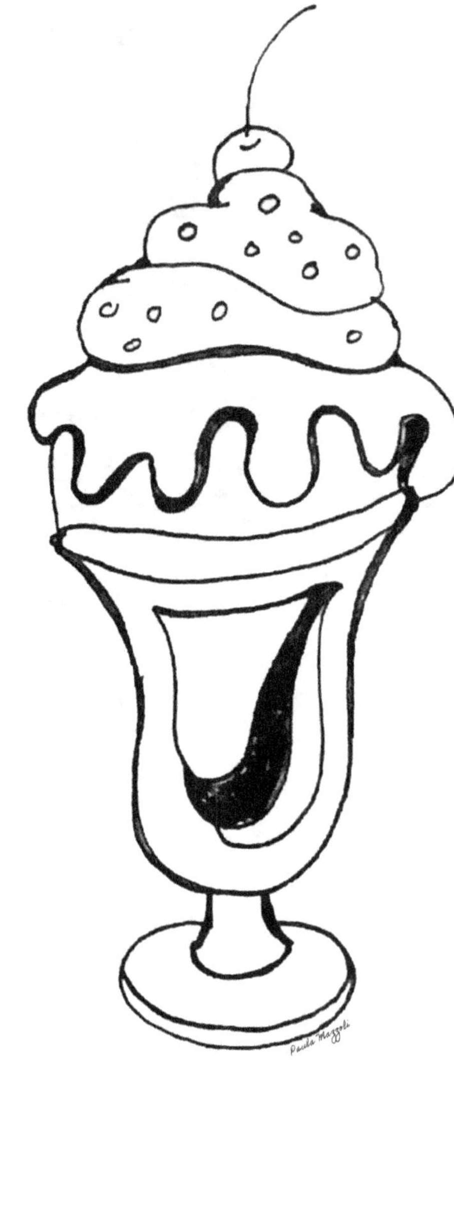

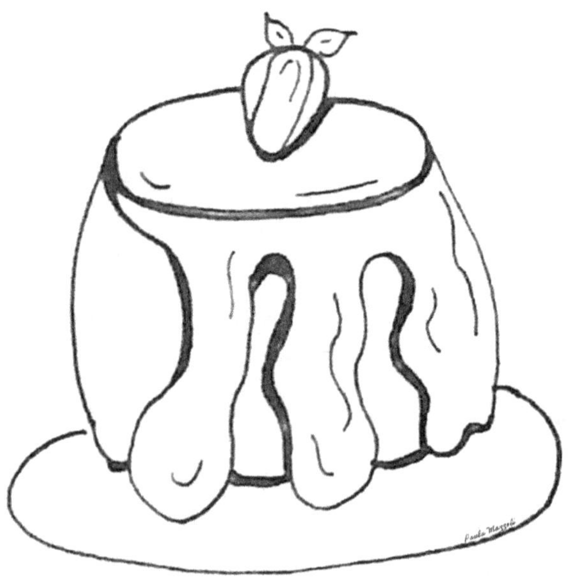

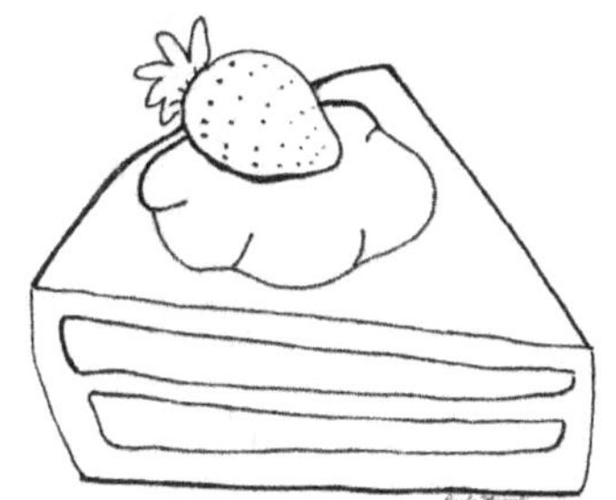

This Coloring Book Belongs To:

____

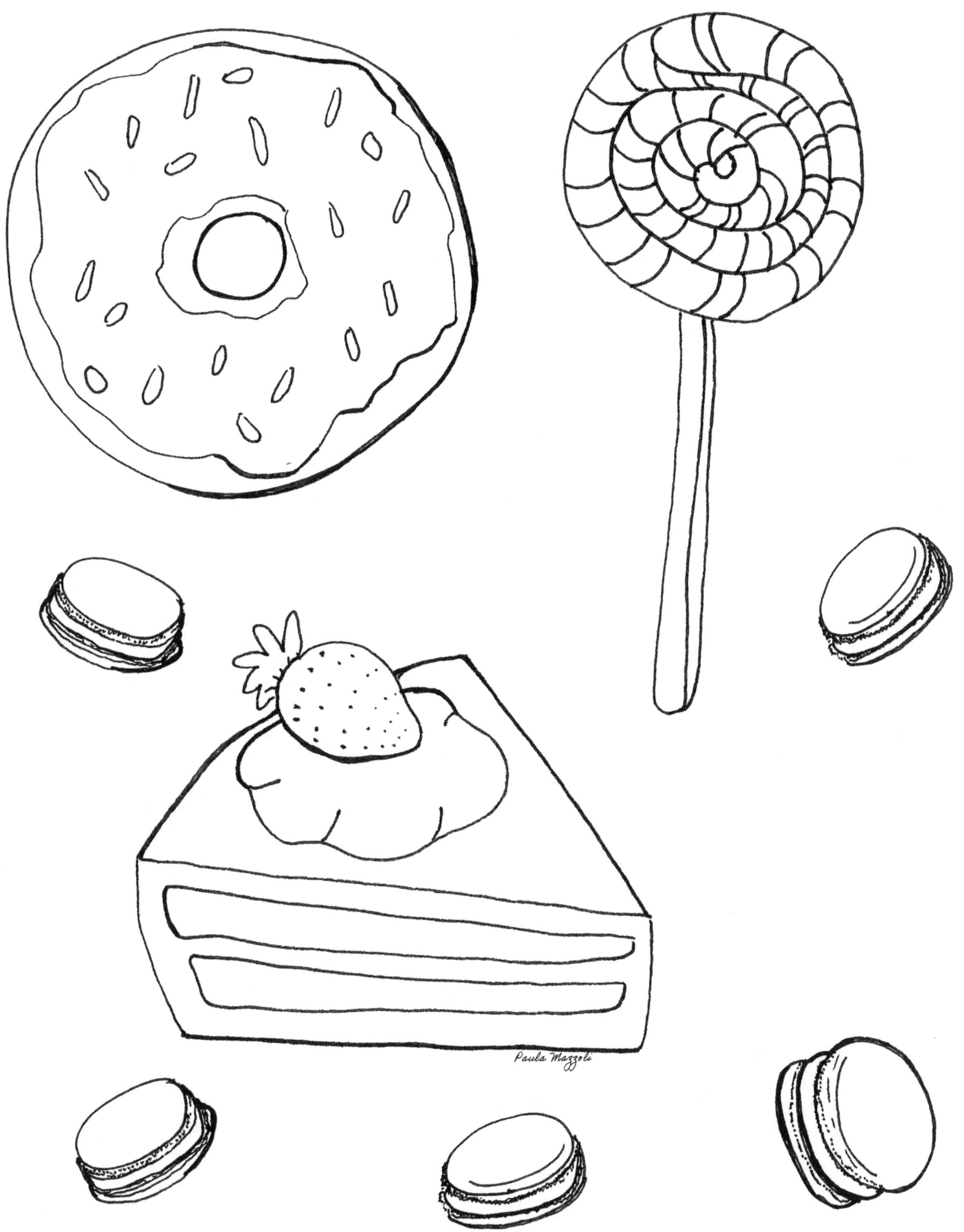
Paula Mazzoli

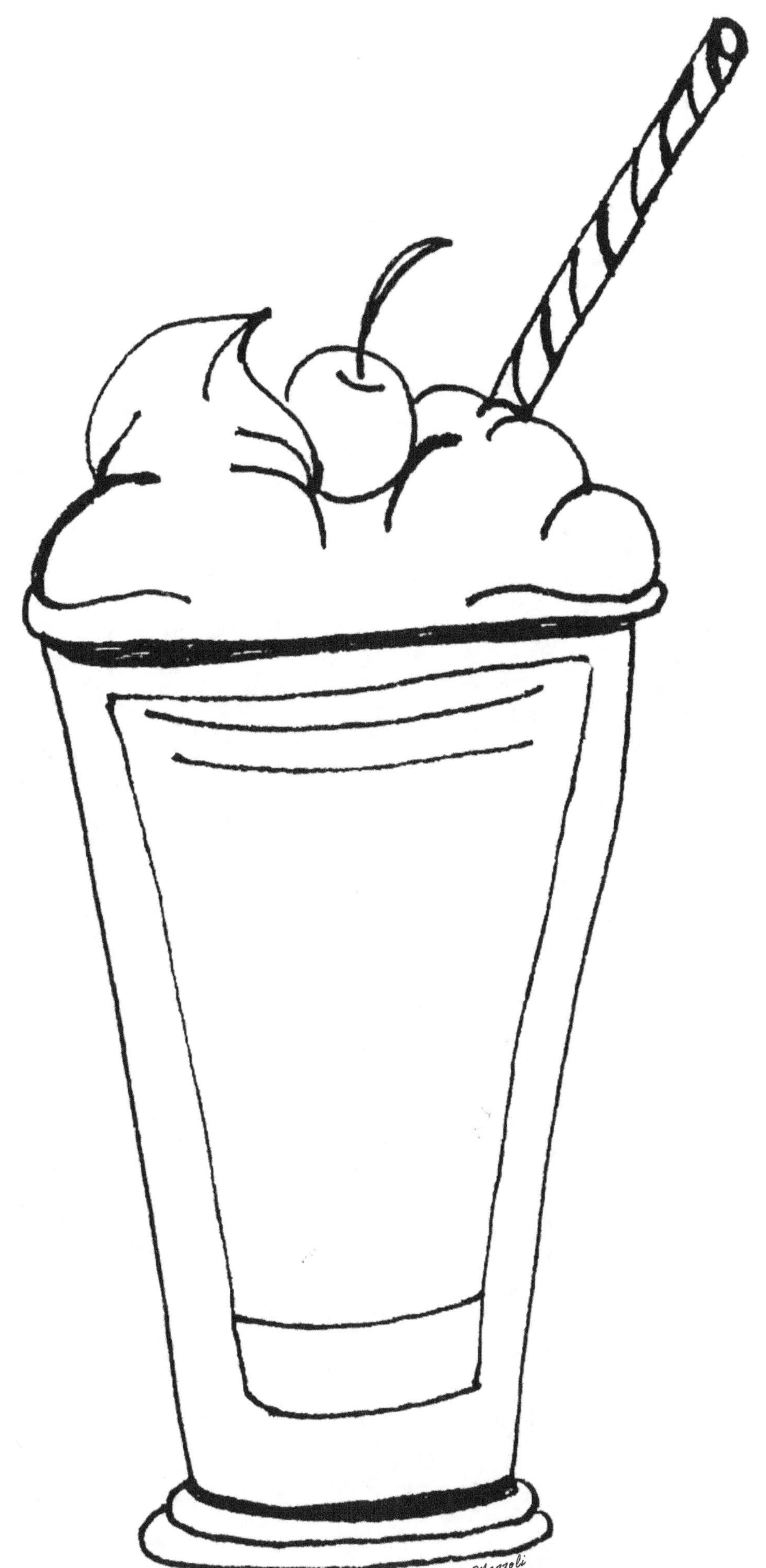
Paula Mazzoli

Paula Mazzoli

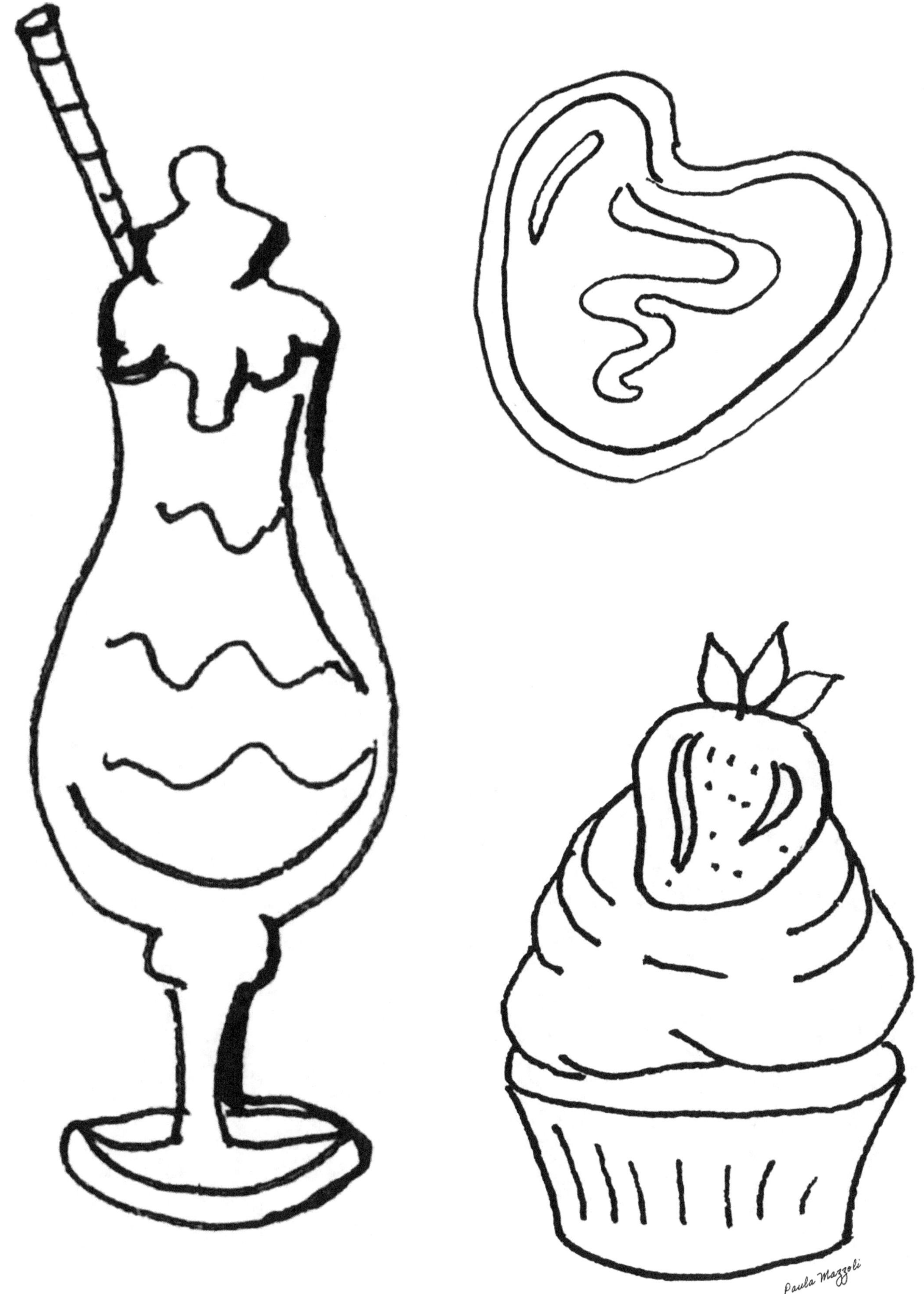

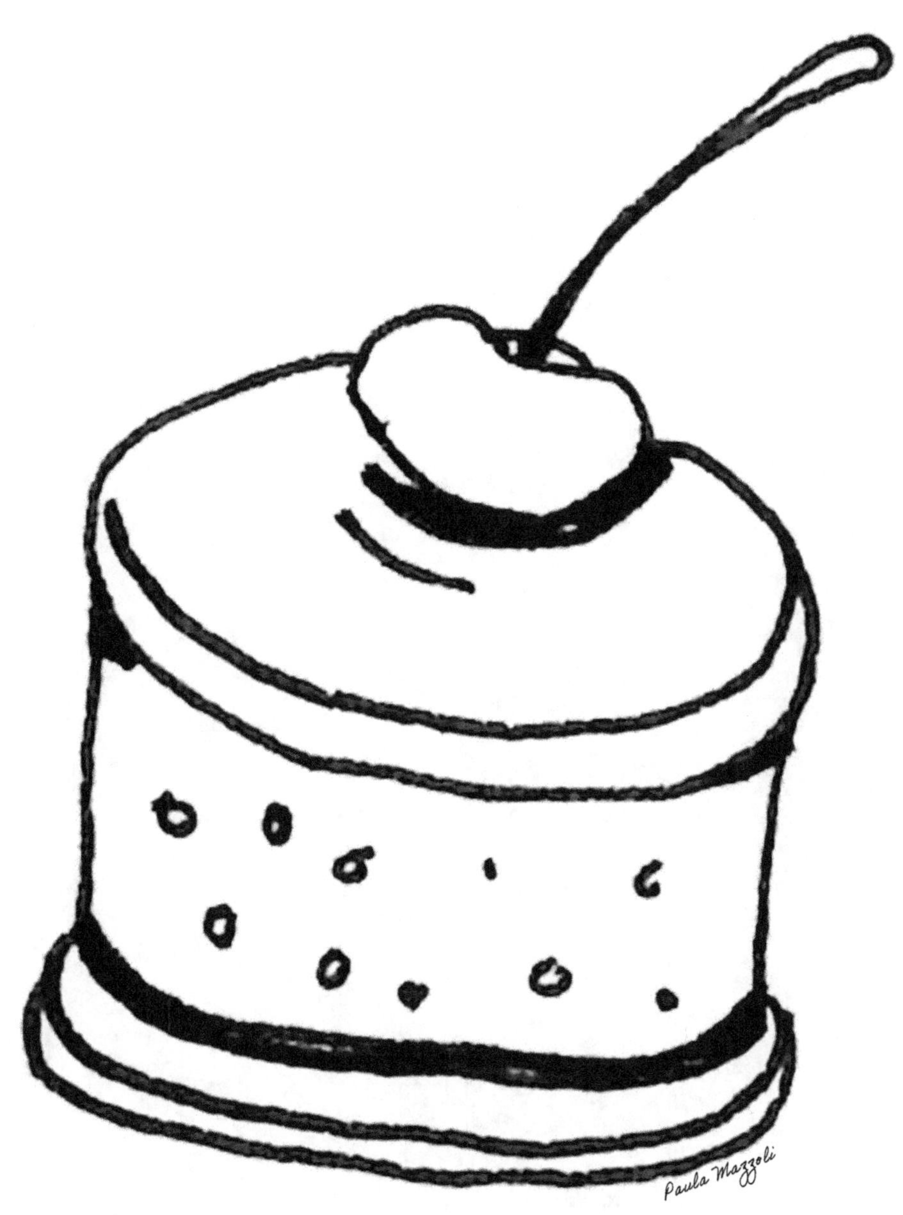

Paula Mazzoli

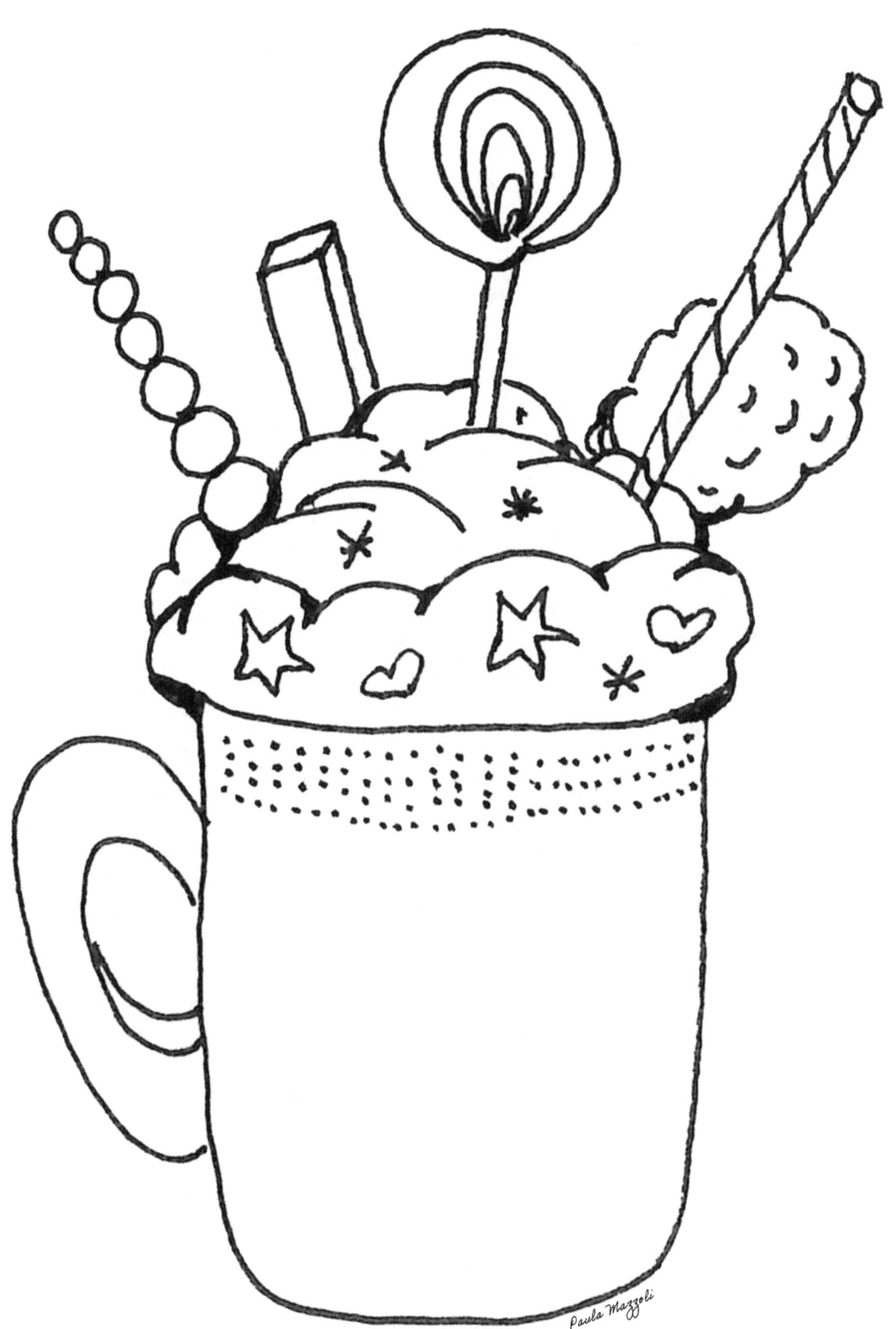

Paula Mazzoli

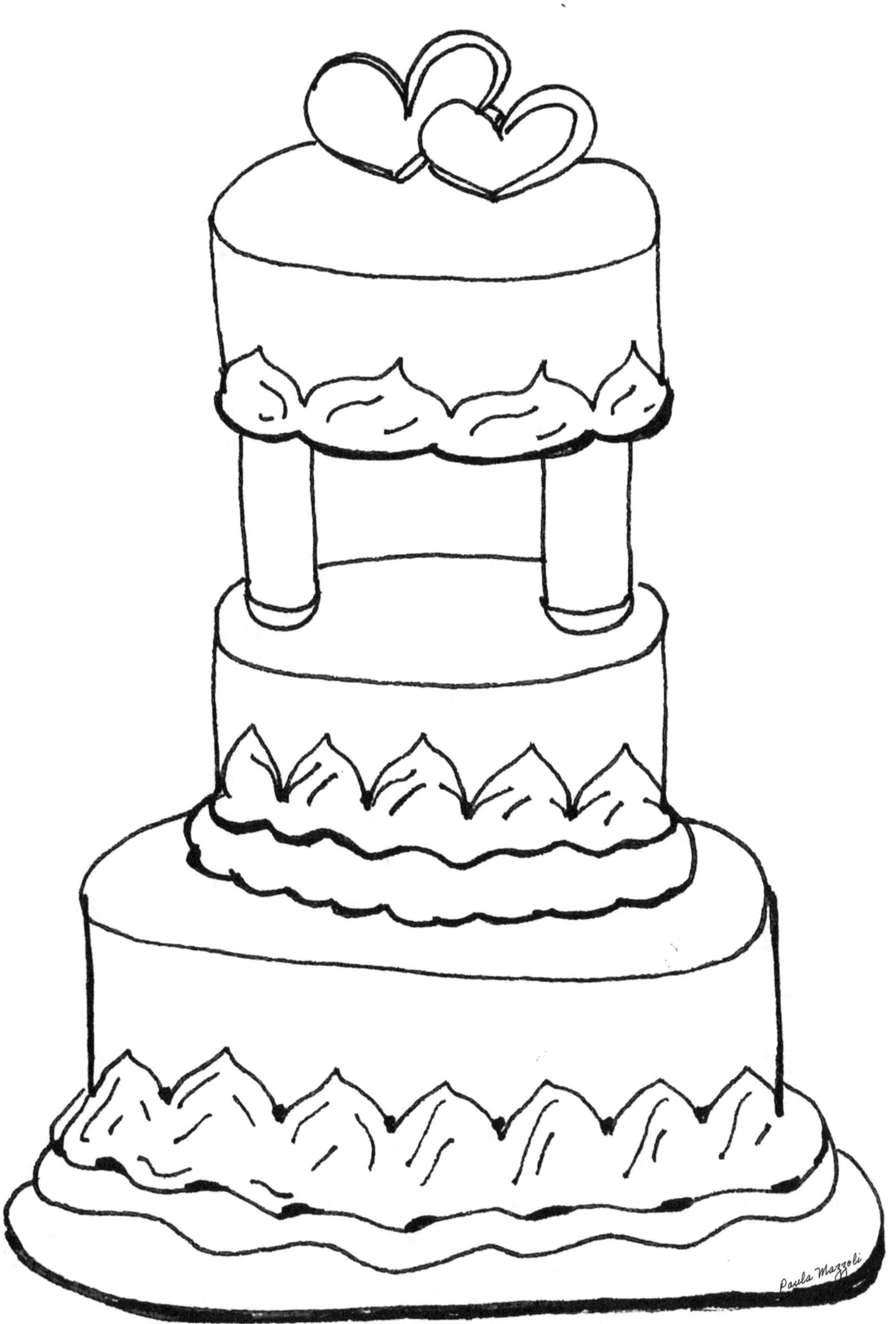

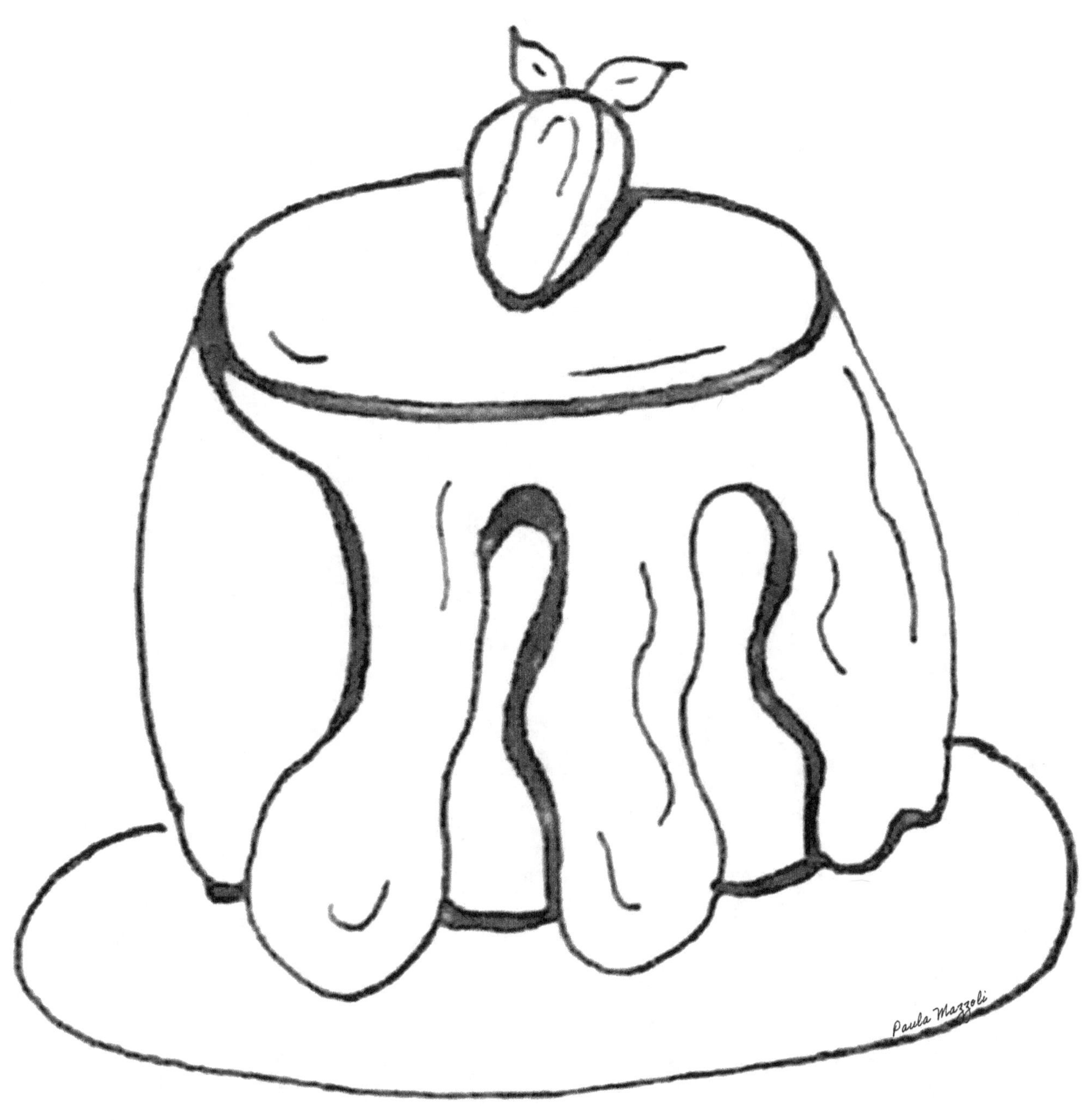
Paula Mazzoli

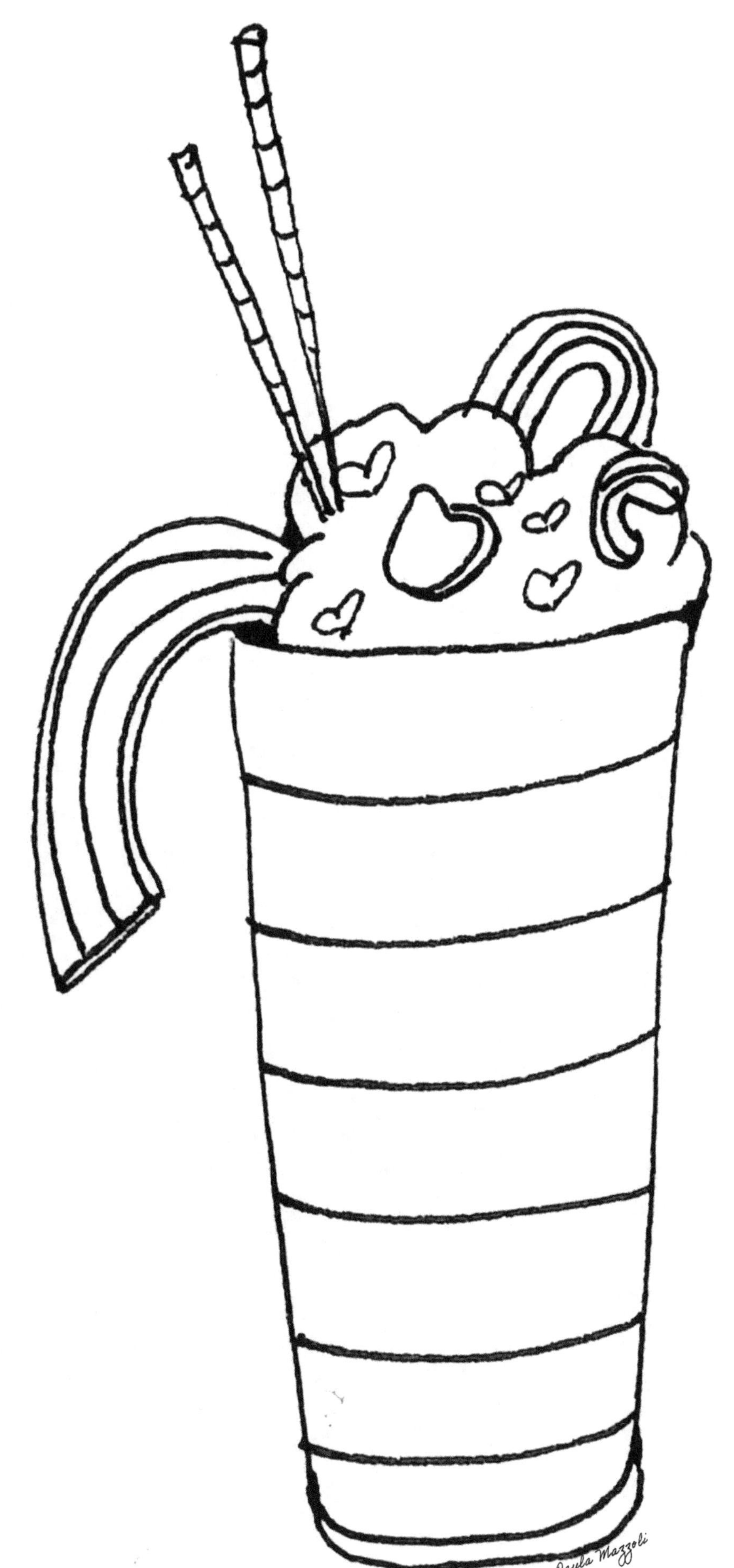
Paula Mazzoli

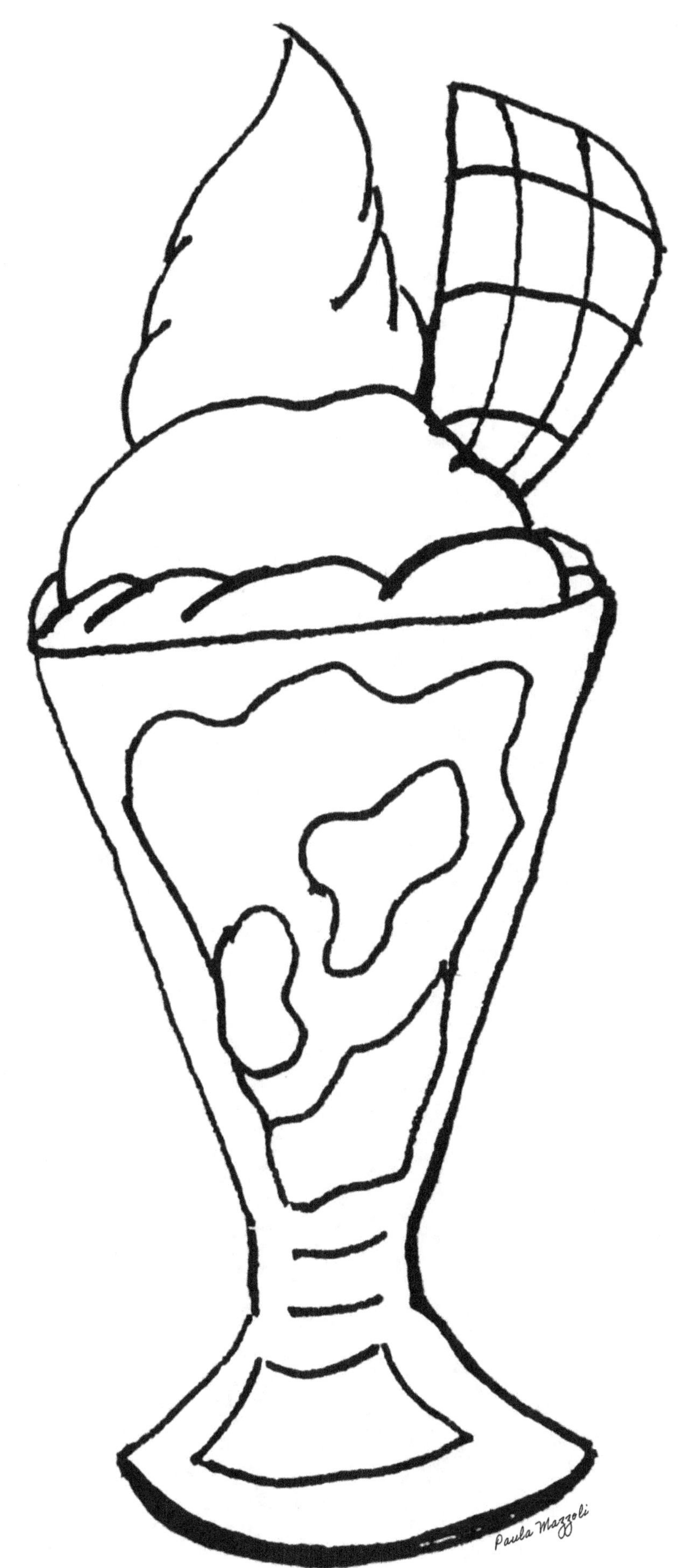
Paula Mazzoli

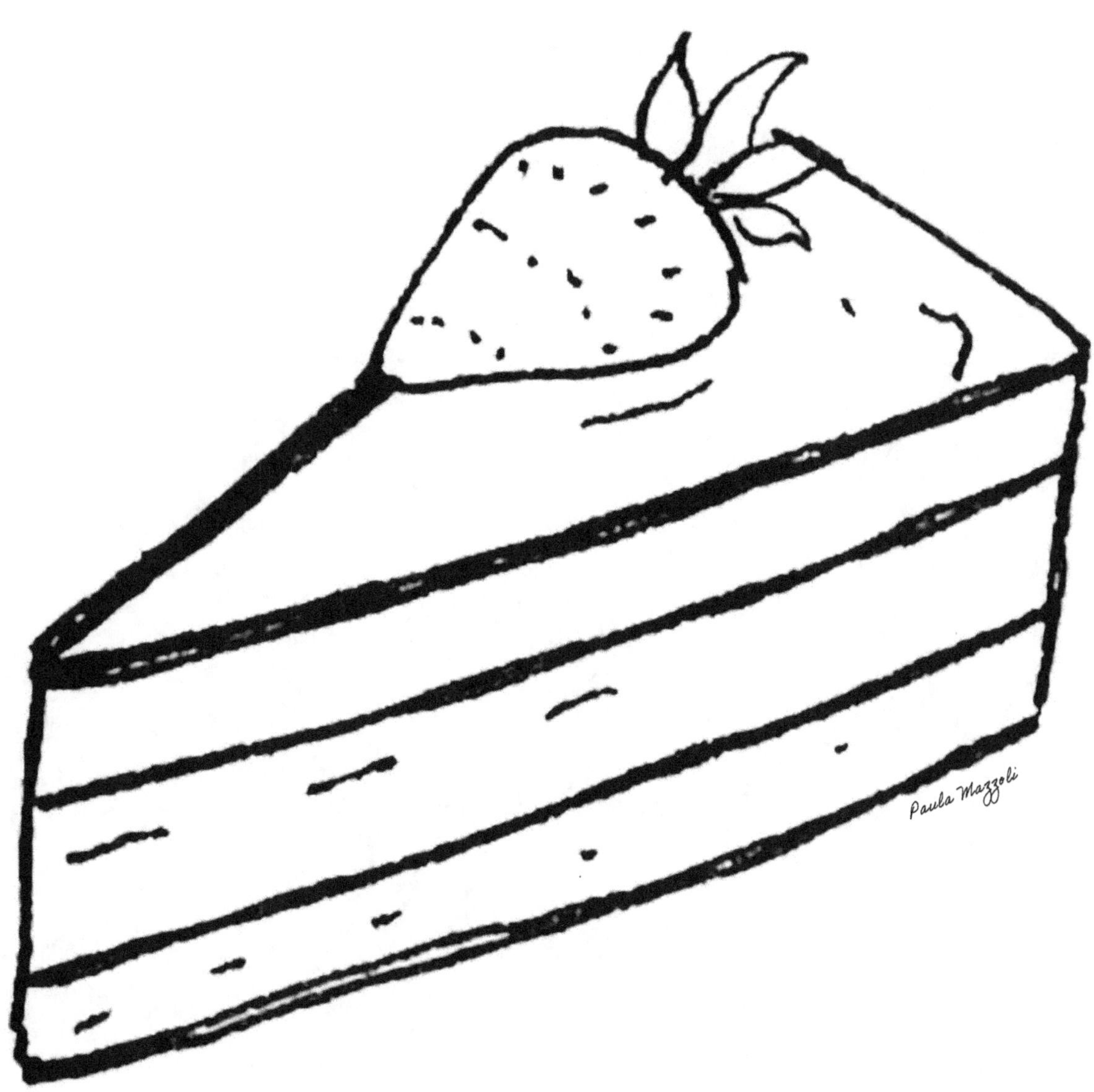

Paula Mazzoli

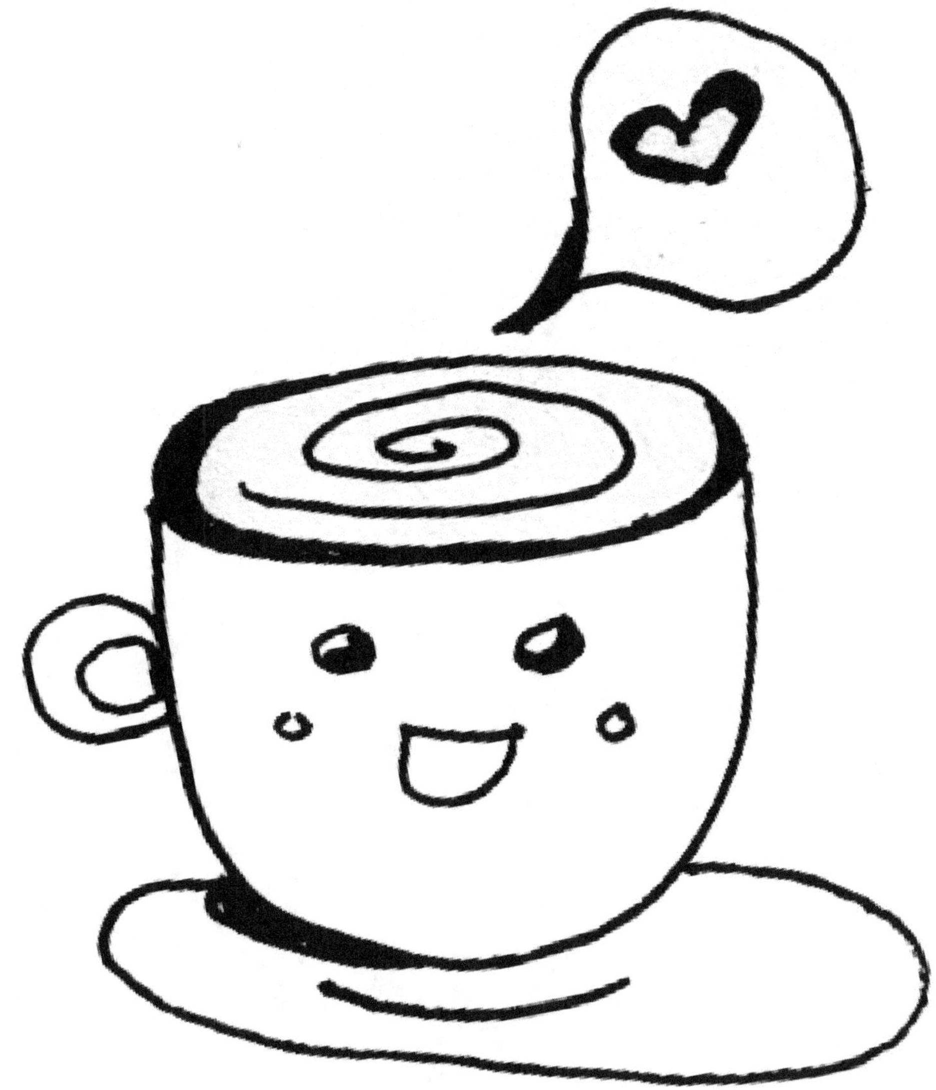

About the Artist

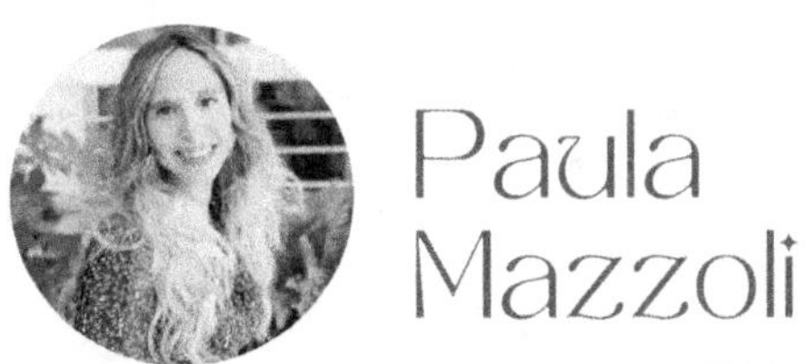

Paula
Mazzoli

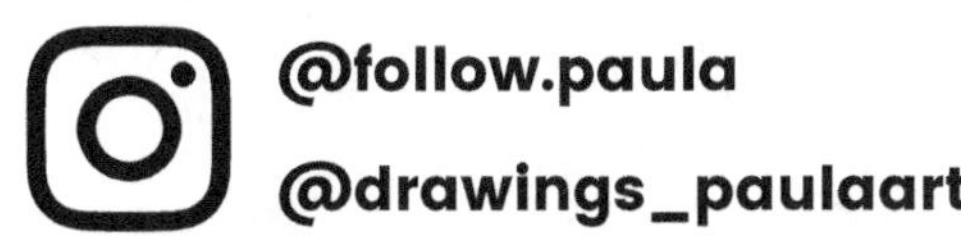
@follow.paula
@drawings_paulaart

Paula Mazzoli is an artist living in sunny California. She works as a marketing coordinator in the Santa Monica office. Paula has an intense background in design. She has a Bachelors Degree in Fine Arts, majoring in Graphic Design. Paula started her career in film and design production by working for top clients such as NBC, E!, CMT, Procter & Gamble, and AstraZeneca. She is also a freelance artist, works in real estate, and loves her dogs.

See more of Paula's artwork: http://pmazzoli.carbonmade.com

www.ingramcontent.com/pod-product-compliance
Lightning Source LLC
Chambersburg PA
CBHW080947260726
48661CB00010B/4137